I am something

The collected writings of

kelly ryan morrison

May 1995

Published in North America by
John Hull Morrison, III
The Piccadilly Printing Company
32 East Piccadilly Street
Winchester, Virginia 22601

ISBN 0-9646000-0-5

Acknowledgments

Grateful acknowledgment is made to Chris Dearing for the cover design, to
Felicia Hart for layout and formatting, and to Lynn Oliver and Kathy Hollen
for graphics contributions.

Contents

Introduction   i

Part One
My Room   1

Part Two
Irruption   63

Part Three
Llama 2   73

Part Four
Smoldering Remains   103

Part Five
Requiem   121

This volume incorporates most of the poems in four volumes issued earlier, included as Parts One through Four. Part Five, "Requiem," consists of new writings not previously published.

All line art illustrations used throughout were created or selected by Kelly for previously printed volumes.

Dates and dedications shown at the end of some poems are included only where Kelly had so indicated.

Introduction

This collection of writings by Kelly Ryan Morrison was compiled and edited by her parents, Joyce Ryan and John Hull Morrison, III. Kelly's writings reveal her passions, her perceptions, and her proclivity for living on the edge. Kelly consistently sought out unorthodox and often risky experiences that promised new sensations and insights. In her 1988 poem "To Want to Write," she said "To experience is to understand...."

She accelerated from one experience to the next, as if to compress as much living as possible into each increment of time. This tendency to live with intensity was also reflected in her activities of choice: horseback riding, downhill skiing, and driving her car.

This same intensity was also apparent in her desire to fulfill a poet's dream – true expression and true art:

> "The life of the poet
> involves a desk
> a paper
> and a want
>
> A want of the eloquent
> to strive for the beautiful
> is the life."

Kelly was able to see behind an image or experience and distill its essence into language. She delighted in summoning the perfect word to express a precise image, and in assembling words in fresh, meaningful ways. She enjoyed sharing the products of her talent. At age eight she wrote, illustrated and bound a series of short verses as a gift to her parents – the first in a series.

Her dedication to the craft of poetry developed steadily. In "Stone Idols" she says "...The passion of other poets is transfused into me." "The Life" sketches a poet's yearning. A number of the entries from the *Requiem* chapter of this book came from a journal she kept in verse every day during her junior year of college.

Nature, animals and personal relationships are the predominant subjects of her poetry.

Kelly's personal style was informal and her preferred setting was outdoors – natural, with sunlight, tall grasses, and animals, especially horses and dogs and most recently, a mule.

She began riding at age five. Over the ensuing years she belonged to the Blue Ridge Hunt Chapter of the United States Pony Club, reaching the second highest level of riding skill (Graduate B). She was trained as a riding instructor and taught riding in Virginia, South Carolina and Georgia. Her intuitive oneness with horses is reflected in the 1993 poem "Tootie":

> "I rode Tootie today
> Slick coat
> Dark liquid eyes
> petite feet
> Brush of mane and tail
> Snappy movements
> Rolicky rhythm
> Soft loving lips
> Nurturing nuzzles."

Another favorite sport was downhill skiing. At age 13, she was lured by the independent nature of the sport, as well as by its companion advantages of speed and access to adventure in exotic places. By age 18, she was winning medals in national slaloms and ranked seventh among women skiers in the state of Virginia. Her 1988 poem "Lift Line Loves" reveals another of the sport's attractions:

> "Into line
> Single? he says
> Sure. Says I
>
> Chair scoops us up
> love begun
>
> Talk of origins
> loves and likes
>
> He goes the hard way
> Still, at the bottom
> as if synchronized
>
> Single? says I
> Sure. He smiles."

Personal relationships were the subject of many of her poems — family, friends, boyfriends, college roommates. For example, "Silvia" speaks of a rite of passage with her best friend while growing up:

> "...we swig berry juice and belch
> two ladies on a saturday night
> puffing and choking
> on what have become brown spitwads
> no matter; we bought them
> (to smoke) so we will
> smilingly suffer through it."

"Strawberry Sun" describes picking strawberries with her grandfather. "Friends in Eternity" talks about hidden feelings for her friend Ryan.

Many poems deal with romantic love. In "Christiaan," she describes the initiation of a summer romance on Hilton Head Island that proved to be critical to her future path:

> ..."Our eyes meet briefly
> and mine lingered
> following, reaching, wondering
>
> I wish to be with him
> on an azure ocean
> or late summer rendezvous."

In a 1993 journal entry, she displays a more mature attitude about relationships:

> "Love is not enough sometimes. You need friendship, caring, respect, compassion, and independence when trying to love someone else and be a part of their life. Just because you love someone doesn't mean that everything will necessarily work out."

Kelly pursued life with zest and passion. She was not content to wait for life's offerings all in good time. Rather she threw herself at life, grabbing experiences out of sequence – now – not later. From these experiences she extracted the maximum pleasure and often pain, and absorbed knowledge that she believed would enhance her next adventure. She succeeded more brilliantly than most at activities that mattered to her, and avoided those that didn't. Throughout, her strong sense of self – of needing to be regarded as unique – was a dominant force:

> "We are nothing
> And in this we are nothing
> Ha!
> <u>They</u> are nothing
> But I -
> <u>I</u> am something."

She acknowledged death in one of her last poems, perhaps intuiting that her own soul's mission would be completed early:

> "If I can stop one heart from breaking
> I shall not live in vain.
> If I can ease one life the aching,
> or cool one pain,
>
> Or help one fainting robin
> onto his nest again,
> I shall not live in vain."

Her spirit was forceful, irresistible, indomitable. Its energy is likely still vibrating around the universe. That spirit was beautifully eulogized by nationally recognized poet Michael Fitzgerald in an original poem read at Kelly's memorial service:

Eulogy for Kelly

"Life as usual was not
in her vocabulary - she was
always in full motion -

when she showed me
her verse, I had to invent
new categories - after all,

the term is "serious poetry"
Kelly was too exuberant,
too vivacious for boxes -
she lived as if life
were downhill skiing -
some people take eighty

years to live two or three
for her - we have lost a treasure -
too soon this candle is put out -

I imagine now that Kelly is
among the stars, sky-writing -
sending us greetings in every shaft

of unleashed sunlight -
no explanation is sufficient -
but we ripen her memory with tears,
laced with joy to have known her.

Michael Fitzgerald
August 5, 1994

Myself

Funny and smart mouth
Loving horses always
Riding all the time.

From *My Gift to You*
Age Eight

Mothers

Mothers are funny
Mothers are very busy
I love my mother
Always taking care of me
My mother is very nice.

From My Gift to You
Age Eight

Part One

My Room

1985 - 1989

Words Upon Wings

standing
I see a paper
flutter
as a butterfly would fly
by

a glimpse caught
of words upon wings

1988

Untitled

Under ice
objects cease movement
yet retain motion

The silence calms
but disturbs the senses

The wish that is carried by the wind
is a burden on my mind

1988

The Life

The life of the poet
involves a desk
a paper
and
a want

A want of the eloquent
to strive for the beautiful
is the life

1988

The Call

When he phoned me last night
My heart blushed
With unspoken emotion
Nonsensical chatter
Each hiding our pent up feelings

I cried

After we hung up
Tempted to call back
I refrain
For fear of being forward
Days go by
and still
cry I

1988
Dave

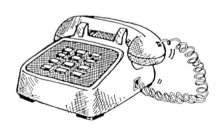

Compared Before

As they have been compared before
Love is like a cobweb
Never fully swept away
It dwells within the hogshead

Full of lies
Full of deception
Full of good times

A fly fills the cocoon
As a spider weaves his web
We fill our own cocoon
With love incomparable
Full, filled, sated
We go on with our lives

Our full, full lives

1988

Anonymous

The smell of hopelessness is in the air
People lined up
The wall in blue chairs
Swinging doors open
All heads swivel
Anonymous name called
Words of consolation
The anonymous trudge into the rain.

Screaming sirens roll
Red Blue White light
Stretcher flys
Excuses
I hear blindly

Family
In chairs over there

Standing by electric doors
With tears in my eyes

1988

A Scene

cool
water
rushes on

trees
nod as
broccoli
stalks
boil
in the hot
sun

yet cool
grass

shining
rocks

a bass
jumps

1988

Thought

Driving by on the highway
On the left, I thought
I saw a lake.

Yet glistening tendrils of grass
Revealed it
as a field

1988
Colorado

Kelly and Jagabar

My Room

Riding

The flashing white
The beating tempo
increases
legs
hurry their way

Tall grass
waving on rough coat

We leave a path
in the gullet high grass

1988

Things To Win

Someone's love
a blue ribbon
that girls hate
Mothers love
an oak plaque
an honorable mention
a bronze medal
a waterbed
a sunburn
New skis
Marvelous Marvin and Hersheys Syrup
First love
a kite

1988

Unthoughts

I reached out to grab them,
But they fell out.
First in clusters,
Then singles.

Until,
I'd no more thoughts in my head.

And I stood there,
With my mouth and brain open,
Thinking nothing

1989

Untitled

We all love
We all run
We all jump
and play
We all wonder
We all cry
We all think
and smile
    (even Grumpy Smurf)
We all abide
We all turn doorknobs
We all hate
We all write
    (inside)
We all wear clothes
We all see
    (colors)

My Room

How To

How to wonder why
to get along
to tie a tie
How to be a Boy Scout
Do you ever wonder
How to
love someone
do buttonfly jeans
be a scientist
write on a blackboard
sit in a chair
go to sleep
How to
write an essay
or
write a poem
or get off a desert island
How to
publish a book
paint a great work
make a clock
or
cook a salad?

My Room

Lift Line Loves

Into line
Single? he says
Sure. Says I

Chair scoops us up
love begun

Talk of origins
loves and likes

He goes the hard way
Still, at the bottom
as if synchronized

Single? says I
Sure. He smiles

1988
Colorado
Carl

The Man On The Moon

The man on the moon,
Has a bad temper.
He smiles,
He frowns,
He laughs,
He cries.
Maybe he causes it to rain
Maybe he makes tornadoes
When he flushes the toilet,
a tornado sweeps everything away.
Maybe Dorothy and Toto
Really went to the moon.
The man on the moon was lonely.

Could you help it?
Being lonely?
So he swept them away,
To keep him company.

Maybe he steals –
all the things
From the Bermuda Triangle
He's just a little lonely!

1988

To Want To Write

How I long to write real poetry
With love in the letters
and heart in the rhythm
a musical piece
From my soul inside
Of green fields
and pink Cadillacs to the prom
Eating lunch on the curb
laughing – grass in our hair.
Of silly names and adorations
Why can't I?
Write?
To experience is to understand
But all that comes
are brief, shallow words
No expression at all.

1988

Moon, Kelly and her trainer, Cathy Frederickson

My Room

My Moon Girl

As I got upon my horse
We began our ride for the worse
I galloped, on that horse of mine
Down that road, in the line
You don't need a whip for Moonglo
All she needs is the wind to blow
All too soon we'll be into town
I'm still trying to slow Moon down
I wonder what my trainer would say
'Cuz I forgot to wrap Moon's legs today
So now my Moon is very lame
My trainer's temper can hardly be
tamed
Back at home, in the barn,
I'm sittin', spinnin' this great yarn.
I wonder who'll believe me now
If I told 'em Moon was a cow?!

1988

Kelly and Moon

My Room

Untitled

Embers glow beneath doe-like skin
Color emitted through minute pores
Kind, plain eyes tell kind, simple love

Stamp on the ground
Eager to be off

Love in speed

faster and faster

like I've never been loved before

1988

Indelible Images

My little friend, impatient hooves stamp firm.
Much love, emitted through soft doelike eyes.
Body as supple, skin as soft as a worm.
Faster, shows her love in speed, I realize.
Coats mixed together; ears flat on bronze neck.
Manes whipping in the breeze; tail a feather.
The tattoo beat of hooves, squeak of leather.
Small animals in the field, fowl awake!
Wind winds through flailing legs, nostrils flare
I love you so – the tattoo screams to me.
The crow calls of too much love – 'Ware-Beware!

Snow falls, tendrils of grass destroyed, of love.
Slowly love subsides, speed wanes, setting sun.

1988
Moon

Maybe

We are nothing
And in this we are nothing
Ha!
<u>They</u> are nothing
But I —
<u>I</u> am something

1989

Outside

I.

I remember
Standing in the streaming sunlight
Rough brick against my cheek
The burnt down grass a dull green
Wondering whether to wear my jeans,
or my skirt,
out that night.
Standing in the falling love
Injurious in its powerful image
Rough love against my heart
The faded relation becoming gray
Wondering whether to leave
or hold fast
after that night

1989
Ben

Outside

II.
I remember
Me and your little sister
Sitting on the
county carnival midway
and <u>she</u>
asked <u>me</u>
what it was like
to be old

1989
Vicki

Routine

Preparing for bed
First take off your Keds
Then off comes your shirt
(Thoughts of the day run)
Slowly brush your hair
(Through your mind-obsessed)
Step in the shower
Slowly lather up
(Events happening)
A fluffy towel
Pools drip on the floor
(Muse about some things)
Then comes your nightgown
Crawl in your cocoon
Childfeet pad bedside –
Goodnight my loved ones
Then you kiss your kids
Then you kiss your cat
Then you fall asleep

1988

Midlife

Standing inside
Before the window
Everyone laughing –
            chatting –
Out the pane
I
Inside in my party dress
Summer sandals
Broccoli bubbling brightly
Smell of fat from the meat,
Permeates every fiber

And the small ones
Outdoors
Trying their wrist at Frisbee

Pasting on my family funny face,
I walk out
Into the blanching sunlight

1989

Kelly with Ryan Royston

My Room

Untitled

Friends in eternity
Us, in my kitchen
Dunking Oreos in lemonade

And he (you) says he wants someone to love
And also love him.

How I long to cry
That I do love him (you).
Words of adulation consume me.

Then he (you) speak of the perfect girl

I –
Old buddy –
Can only gawk
Speechless
At your blindness

1989
Ryan

Frolicking

Busy lights
As their blueness
Flickers slowly
Searching

For beauty on the crowded midway

Then a blueness
As true as thine own

They meet and introduce
They flit, and titter as schoolgirls

Doing a coy dance
to
and
fro
Behind curled lashes

1989

Mindfulness

The laden fog
Carries no boundaries
To my
Fantasy soaked mind

I open
Into a realm
Beyond which
I cannot exceed

And again
I stutter
      stagger
To full realization

Of purpose

1989

My Room

Waves

The subtle copulation
Of wind and water
Grains of mist
Touching every part of the universe.

The simple joining
Of two people
Effervescence of love
Seeing the population

1988
Hilton Head, SC

Untitled

Mane whipping in the stillness,
Through the shine,
of the sun.
Brisk steps,
On recently saturated earth.
Spongy life underfoot..

We run.

'Till heaving, both
Return peacefulness
Only hoofprints to remind us

1989
Moon

Leopard

Lithely
Mottled movements in the bushes
Slide by the
minds eye

And you see
Copper on black
Gold and red, in
A smooth slink. Past
your eye.

Through the lush jungle growth,
Green drips from the senses.
And the silence
overwhelms.

1989

Untitled

It had seemed
An endless conquering of spirits

She sighed
As his hands went over her body

1989

Animals

In the night they come
to haunt you
Their small grisly faces
Smiling in wanton agony

To throttle you
for chewing on their ears
at age 3

To scratch out your retinas
for throwing them
in an adolescent skirmish
at age 13

With the rhythm of your
nighttime breathing
Their slow procession advances
over
The rainbow stained sheets

1989

Ugly

Excitement:
Bellowing its nervousness,
From the small childs face.
As the cellulite in the
Mothers thighs –
Barely contained,
jiggles.
The child jumps up and down,
tugging on polyester.

The child bounds ahead,
and the woman,
in yellow –
(S-T-R-E-T-C-H)
shorts,
follows laboriously.

1989

In A Field

abandoned truck
rust and faded
shattered glass
shattered heart
grass grows
fender deep
as knee deep love

a man
turns
sees
shrugs

One day,
that man, with shattered heart,
and knee deep love
thinks of that old truck

His tears fall
as intricacies in the dust

1988
Steve

Teen Ski Bus

The aimless lull of rubber on
asphalt
The sharp, tangy taste
The blaring thought in my head
The pull of an octopus' tentacles,
As they tear from barnacled granite.
The acrid smell of wood burning
The fine line, between suspicion
and doubt

1989
Killington, Vermont

The Swinger

Scuffing up the porch steps
I look past the yard
over the fence
to the familiar, forgotten
tire swing

And again
   – as always –

My feet are pushing
Hair streaming
Hands rebelling against rough rope
Creaking limbs over head.

So I turn to open the door
Until next time.

1989

Forever Felt

Janis, wailing about Bobby McGee
My neck cricked, to pull the thread
Of the small flower
On the bra I'm wearing
and we're laying
in the green tranquility
of my room.
Furniture lost.
Paradise traced

and the mirror tells
Of us
in our underwear

And us
in the permanence
of that night

1989
Silvia

Shafts of Autumn Light

Sometimes I wonder where the greening goes,
As summer falls, with nineteen tumbling leaves.
The farmer, with his horse and big plow, mows.
Power. Against the collar the horse heaves.
A harvest moon glows red over the land.
Too quickly go the bullet-like clock hands.
Chlorophyll goes, red shows through, greening
gone.
The rivers flow, soon snow, the farmer plows.
Will the fourth crop be in? He knits his brows,
With the first rays of light – spot coated fawn.
On the edge of the field, he lays to rest.
Watchful mother, white flag on the alert.

Horse, in his collar and plow. Deer his quest.
The greening goes, toilers silhouetted.

1989
Valentines Day

You

Loitering in English
I suddenly smile
because
I'm thinking of you

I thought of
(the hay bales
the tables at the shop
my couch
your car)
Those places we loved each other

Tearing in English
My eyes suddenly fill
Because
I thought of you

1989
Stevie

10 AM

Return Blackness
Engulf me in your sameness
Innumerable parts
Identical shares
In Darkness
I am cast
in the play
Of consuming Night

1989

Untitled

I.

Confusion
Is the unknowing blackness
Of utter oblivion
And I fall, into this
vacuum
Arms and legs flailing
Helplessly
Against the tug of hurt
Pain
That I know will come
But the jolt doesn't reach me
Instead —
I spin past words and feelings
Alas —
Circles
Until thoughts become
Mass chaotic revelation
No true conclusion at all

II.

Then a deduction is reached
And I skip
Into the moonlight
Rightness reverberating repeatedly
Until I spin on purpose
For the thrill
Of
Purposeful confusion
Then reality smacks me.
Like a pinch out of a dream
My arms out for balance

Twirling
I turn again and again
Adrenaline like acid through my veins
I tire
And cease
Hearing and sane now

III.

I lay spreadeagle on my back
In the humming of earths rotation
The beeslike carnival goers on a midway
My nose
Has an almost indiscernible bit of pollen on it

My saucers try
To focus on it – to no avail

I rest
My mind enveloped in the spin
My body caught in confusion
The meadow rolling like a huge waterbed
And the sky
Is a blue and grey and white tie-dye
I fancy I see a rabbit

1989

I Still

After he leaves
I can still smell:
his cologne on my clothes
his breath in my hair

I can still feel:
his caress on my cheek
his hand at my side

I can still taste:
his lips on mine
his powerful aura

I can still see:
our browns and blondes mixed
and the floral of the cushion

Of the couch
my mother has
downstairs

1988
Stevie

Stone Idols

When asked who
was my idol?
I answered craftily,
What weight do you place
on this person's shoulders?
Some – was the equally crafty answer,
To what (or whom) do I attribute my passion?
A stone figure from an Aztec culture?
A picture of J.F.K.?
No –
The passion of other poets
is transfused into me

1989

Monotony

...is the endless gridwork
of a busy city
...is the numbing wave
of a foot, in mid-air
...is a baby's constant wail
searching for attention
Monotony
...is the pigeon in the park
begging for crumbs
...is the gravel
beneath my feet
...is the tempered, aimless lull
of tires on asphalt
...is the bark of a tree
gnarled and brown
Monotony
...is the small minority
of everyday being

1989

Labor Day

Last day of summer
So we bitch and moan
And laze in the just cut grass
The last of the sluggish flies
Buzzing
In our school cut hair
Then it's time
We heave ourselves upwards
And wish to stay in summer
Eternally –
My dinner's ready
So you cross the street
Summer's over

1989

Nodding Heads of Wheat

Black children stood in the fields
Faces turned toward expectant sky
The fire queen reigned
Their cheeks pregnant with berries
Cotton forever shimmering in the sun
Hopeful hands find each other
Subjects under the hazing sky
While the billowing clouds piled
on one another
These children stand in embrace
Under the dying queen's throne

1989

The Snapper

She moves into the room
Paid no heed

She announced to the room
"It's a turtle"
And the wait.

"In a box" she says
THEN they gather round
Oblivious.

The turtle glares at the row of impudent faces
Who are maddeningly baneful

1989
Old Dominion Animal Hospital
McLean, Virginia

Small Surprise

The snow whipped across the slope
looping its leaping lash
around trees and rocks
We hiked
Rocks were our path
We, like billy goats
Skis, boots on our backs
We hiked
a swig of water, here.
To diminish salty sweat.
We hiked
to the top

Bliss
We carved slow slinky "S" turns
Down the ravine
We skied
Stop! to rest
We sat on a rock
To watch others go by
In slow, slinky "S" turns
and then –!
a man came skiing very fast
Down that very steep crevasse
and off flys his leg
Oh! we gasp

He calmly reaches down
to pick it up
and strap it on again

1988
Tuckermans Ravine
Mt. Washington, NH

Superhighwarp

Along a dark freeway
Yellow lines from below
FLASHING
At my face
Beams of stealthy light
Night prowlers
to my left
Fast
and I see the passageway
to freedom
Green fields on poles
Quartz arrows point

I slow to allow
for warp speed to brake down

Escape

I Flintstone it
to a string of lights
and wait

1989
Stevie

Picture of Her

She stared at me,
With the blank look of a Victorian portrait,
Flat, cool powder
on puffy skin
Like gallium,
She became smolten under my gaze
Oozing from sight
Still her still eyes are affixed
and my eyes narrow further
as she floats away in a gust of artificial air
Mimicking fierce ventilation

Marshall, VA

a millisecond
driving through a country
"The boys"
leaning against a pickup
down at the Handy-Mart
Children
playing under a tree
mother snaps with an Instamatic
girl
holding her stomach, in a doorway
crying to a boy.
Silt lays in the gutters
like ashes of generations gone by
We tool out of town,
broad expanse of asphalt before us.

1989
Marshall, VA

Part Two

Irruption

1990

Riders

The mournful wind dove curiously
over the grassy apex of the hill.

Our buoyant steps lose
their individuality…
become a single, universal trail
through the meadow.

We light upon a small mound
pause to gaze at the surrounding rocks,
Then warily turn toward
the last meniscus of sun.

About to betray the casual
onlookers, it disappears
g r a d u a l l y …
leaving us unfulfilled,
desiring to feel again
the splendorous glow

of true, natural genius.

Friends in High Places

The vacant road,
and faint wetness,
creep imperceptibly
around me, surrounding me;
It prepares me

as I nod,
shut my eyes,
and die.

Shadows

When the sun came over the curve of the Earth,
The fence gave birth to a monster.

It stretched and devoured the field,
Tried to consume the oak boards.

Silvia Costales and Kelly

Silvia

smoking el producto cigars
by porchlight on my deck
making a hand signal code
to tell each other about last
night so my sleeping parents
wouldn't hear
and talking about your dad
in cuba when he was fifteen
smoking havana cigars
playing groucho marx
down to the eyebrows

we swig berry juice and belch
two ladies on a saturday night
puffing and choking
on what have become brown spitwads
no matter; we bought them
(to smoke) so we will
smilingly suffer through it.

Christiaan

Tan feet dance on the non-slip
Soapy suds frolic about
The Hero shines in the harbor sun

Other mates finishing the day

Our eyes meet briefly
and mine lingered
following, searching, wondering

I wish to be with him
on an azure ocean
or late summer rendezvous

(l. to r.) Christiaan Pollitzer, Phil Smith, Kelly, Kathy Jonkers

Untitled

The wailing of the old Kunah
indian medicine man pierced
everything around our nakedness.
The foamy spray spuming
over the trash on the beach
blinded my eyes, attracted
to your broad olive back.
The luminescent moonbeams alight
on my fingers, halting their
path to your delicate curls.
The hearty mumbling of the
indian pigs drowns out the
sound of my marred, grieving heart.

Part Three

Llama 2

1991

The Ascent

We left the road, for
a log-lined path, around
boulders, over a bridge, through
leaves and broken twigs.

Your sneakered feet in front of me
guiding me through the perils:
logs, stones, and bugs.
Showing me the way to the top.

We pull a branch aside to pass…

Shakedown

into the campsite.
Two hearths, a lean-to;
rocks to sit on; a
tree to rest against.

The lush canopy muffles
all noise.

Except our breath.
And the babbling brook,
where the stream
comes out…

The Wishing Well: Where the Caterpillars Go To Die

near an old above ground well
crumbly and stony.
We perched on the edge,
and peered into the interior.

But tiny corpses of fuzzy ones
distract us. In different
stages of rigor mortis
they lay all over, and on top of,
the wall.

We pick up our backpacks,
and, shuddering, strike out…

The Ledge

for the lichen covered cliffs.
You helped me up the steep parts,
we climbed together.
We reached the summit, and
rolled up our shirtsleeves.

Roasting, basting in our sweat,
we spied a hawk in flight
First near us, then
over the tree tops.

We danced on the precipice...

The Descent

soon we tired, and departed the rocks.
Slippidy slid down
through the loamy debris.

We thought we saw an owl,
but it was only shadows,
so we continued.

WEE-OOO meant you were falling.
LOOK-OOK-OOK meant
that you had found something.

Soon we crossed the bridge again,
and went back to the road...

The Bath

Before leaving, though,
there happened a small water war.
Our feet were numb
hair dripping, soaking,
clothes wet with sweat and water.

You put a tape in the car radio,
we splashed and played
like two kids oblivious

Untitled

Where will we be without him?
To trust, to count on, to love.
The web surrounding us is gone.
The hope he gave us,
the values he taught us,
cannot disappear;
We can't let them.

When kids go to school,
When there's no lying,
stealing, wronging;
He'll give that grin and smile
Because we're doing him right,
Like he did us.

He wasn't faultless,
But now we have to try to be.
That's what he wanted.

We all love you Chinaman;
Christmas will never be the same.

Daughter of Spain
(Hija de Espana)

Gracefully she walks
    (camina)
Her black skirt blowing
      (la falda)
The wind lifting it
    (levantandola)
Full lips, white teeth
      (blancos)
Smiling, taking in the sights
       (vistas)
She glides by, slowly
      (despacito)
I can only imagine her
     (imaginarla)

Routines

Eyes squinted against the smoke
a cigarette
slanting white across his chin

Hand trembling on the glass
a martini
eating at his black consciousness

White death moving floorward
clear Fate heading mouthward
eyes squint, hands tremble

Untitled

I haven't been writing for awhile.
Don't seem to be words
or even feelings;
just (now) blocked out memories
of a half-eaten bacon sandwich
certain laugh or squint

Can't cry anymore
all seems distant.
Except there's still love
when I say that name –
or more often think it

And then there are fallen hopes
broken hearts, torn desires
more violence, hatred
stemming from the one time:

The true soldier lay
    half in
        half out
The Gates of Heaven.
peace China.

Eulogy

For himself and for us
He lived and fought
Let hope carry us now
He was our soldier
May God rest his soul.

for Chinaman

One Night

sittin' on the horsey on the
downtown mall
hopeful expectant to
see your face over
the picket gate
laughing wanting to
keep the moment
alive forever

Kelly with Kathy Jonkers at Hilton Head

Us

You say I never write for you
But in my pent-up mind
thousands of lines
of all we've gone through

Nothing comes out
like it's supposed to
So, unworthy, it retreats
to the memory place

beaches mustangs beers
men horses streets
lifeguards kooshballs
rapping singing (trying)

These are mine
never touched nor tainted
This is us

Infinity

Out of control
a spinning top
that can't stop
a loose hubcap
on an open road
seeds of wildflowers
dropped in a field
a stray hockey puck
skidding on ice
a Slinky
on a flight of stairs
a teenager's drug-
crazed stupor
the twenty-three hour
blackness of Alaska
The sight of someone
slowly dying
that can't stop crying

Meteor Shower

Smelling the sounds
feeling the sights
cigarette hand chilled
acrid smoke blowing away
wetness of the ground
soaking through shirt
and pants
waiting for a shower

Red hot crystals
smaller

than a grain of sand
flaming through us
then vanishing.
Suddenly forgotten.

Standing up
cold hands
      butt
           feet
          back
I see one.

Writing Aids

I live in my Thesaurus
To try to find normal words
To say wonderful things
About great people
And fun stories.

To use words to tell a tale
or get across a point
To not be trite, and cliche
or common, everyday.

To be unique, sole, matchless,
single, unequaled, alone,
peerless, rare, singular, exotic,
solitary, and unsurpassed.

So I won't sound bad.

The Vault

Gyrating, twisting, churning
Music pulsing, spurring
Bodies in staccato flight.
He can almost see the light,

From the outside shining in –
to the pit of dancing sin,
Where tormented youth gone wild,
Nature's curse, the child

Rose above the streaming mass,
To try to break Heaven's glass.
So shattered it into shards,
Onto the faces upturned in the yards,

Of Surrey, Gorky, and Central Park.
Shafts of light shine through the dark,
Onto the consciences of the youths,
On the dance floor, in drugstore booths

Freed from tracing the trodden path,
Thus incurring Satan's wrath.
The evils in them diminished at last,
The stripling's flag flies at full mast.

Kelly and her paternal grandfather, John Hull Morrison, Jr.

Llama 2

Strawberry Sun

Grandfather and I picking strawberries
It was always June
early June
And he would roll up his work khakis
While I wore my bathing suit

All you could pick for six dollars
We went for the day
all day
And he would pull them off the stems
While I popped them into my mouth

It was a long walk to the car
From the back of the patch
a big patch
And he would carry both the berries and me
While I nodded off on his shoulder

For Naught

Our values wave on top o' the flagpole
Unerringly, we cherish them, believe'n it
But follow it for what? Values he stole
By killing our youth; the people he hit
with a blow so hard, we couldn't recover
Fate has left us, just pain and hate now
Patriotism easily smothered
So, my old friend, take a deep bow.
You destroyed our country, forever
Sacrificed our youth, we know for naught
They lay still, heads, bodies severed
No, the faith is gone, it can't be bought
The people are sick of being run over
By a leader whose burden is too big for
    his shoulders.

Untitled

I love the smell of you
mixed with me
exuding from my pores
a sort of odorous inspiration
sweet, tangy, chewy

Clear as gin, but tastier…
to my deep regard:
for your ability to
impassion me with flavor;
fill me with two people;
devote yourself to me;
adore me unadulterated;
wholly enchant me.

If just one cell of you
stays in me, stays alive
I will be content.

Alma Mater

Though some of us just got here,
Others have been here for years.
It's now time for us to part;
together, in tears.

Planning, arranging, waiting,
for days to yet go by;
Soon we'll all unfold our wings,
and then we'll learn to fly.

Seems as though it'll never end,
Twelve years working for –
a ceremony we'll all attend,
then turn, and close the door.

Reunions will come and go,
Faces and names will change.
We may not see each other much,
But Handley will remain.

So go, class of '91,
I'll miss you but not remember.
Unfortunately things will fade,
Walking up those steps forever.

Class graduation poem
1991

Fire

Just one more time…
Please, God. Please can I?
Her parched white lips said.
Tears roll freely down her face.
She did, now she's dead

A nice house. Expensive
antiques in niches
Their hands groping for
escape to a holy reefer world.
They did, behind closed door

dirty alleys, Hills homes
no one escapes
just moans and groans
of how to stop it?
how to fight?

Can't close the door
on blackest night.

"The Brat Pack"
Sarah Deutermann, Kim Hansen, Kelly, Kathy Jonkers,
Sally Ohlidal, Jenny Bledsoe, Sarah Pillion.

Part Four

Smoldering Remains

1992 - 1993

Kelly with "Sisty" Rebecca

Dentist's Appointment

How it must feel
(Open up W I D E R –)
to peer into
the C   M
    H   S
      A
of orality

Gardens

The matrimony
of the sun and the dirt
and the rain
gave birth to twelve
red sons, bursting
from behind yellow
wooden stakes,
still
clinging to their nannies'
jagged green skirts —
embarrassed for their
obscenely luscious
verdancy

Untitled

It's late
and the
rain
in fat beads
mottled
red
white
black
flickering
strands
of vision
bang on
one thought:
Reba
and the butcher
crying
lilting
stirring
meshing
gnashing
devouring

Untitled

I love to see you
clinging to me
tendrils
on my flushed chest
follicles of life
creating their own movement
winding, weaving
through my soul
interlocking and enjambing
cells atoms particles
reflecting lust
in the shiny glass

Psychology

New car, nervous laugh
Rolling along, riding alone
Together to class,
Chatting of changing scenery,
Many buildings, more than ever
All over. Anything but
Pretty. Your person excites me
invites me, intrigues me.

Untitled

They run in a herd
shaggin along
a motley crew
swishing through the
high meadow on
red claycrete
the road black
as dirt unfolds
alongside their yard
clipped short by
yellow teeth of
nannies, pink
gums of kids
gnawing on Queen
Anne's Lace

On Growing

Wisdom or lecture
I could not say
only conjecture
if I may
as to the nectar
which I missed
Blanking out
leaving you dismissed
I'm thirteen now
I can't be kissed
no more. Let me go
Take a bow
your job is complete
I'm full of morals,
head to feet.

Untitled

Oh! To get the bills paid,
And to have enough to keep the maid.
Never need to pick up a spade
Stroll around bedecked in jade
Sipping a glass of lemonade
A new dress when the old should fade
Never fear! We got it made!

Wouldn't it be nice
if I made thrice
of that which I make now?

Webster My Friend

Ever smell an old book?
Open a big old book
you haven't opened for
awhile
and breathe in the
faint mothballs
formaldehyde
– generations of life
and almost get high
off of it.
Maybe olfactory osmosis
time and world religion
consumed by inhaling

Untitled

there's a gaiety in the air
Time has not yet
poked His scaly head around
the corner
green abundancy towers
overhead, wafting
scents of rutting musk
earthy delight
and hybrids of mushrooms
loamy soil

then He lumbers as a
slow turtle
fat and round, full
of years

engulfing them, their homes
leaving a clean swatch
of clipped cropped
stubble.

Untitled

The road split the trees
so the clouds
and burnt sky
could come through

I spin over
intervals of orange
yellow dashes
into the shivering
sky
of Georgia winter

26847

Going to visit my great
grandmother
in the nursin' home
Four generations
Every Sunday
Interminable hour

At first
when I was little
She rocked me
Spoke longingly
of fording the creek
sidesaddle
riding her white horse
to school

Then when I
got older
– and she also aged –
the smell
of incontinence
and liniment
pushed me back
into the hall

Untitled

ponies paint
red & white
overo ponies
grazing stomping
lazing like ponies
in a field
of dandelions
red clay
blurs
rosecolored sight
of ponies
red & white
in dandelions

Carter Hall 1993

Crackers in my pocket
flask filled with sherry
tie tied tight
pony smartly braided

Steam rises from sweat
on carefully clipped coats
sturdy legs beat staccato
with asphalt on borium

Chasing hounds, myths
of social acceptance
Pink coats, nostril linings
Flapping and heaving

Stubble underfoot, hard
nimble toes scramble
approach and lift
over the rough stonewall

Smoldering Remains

Kelly and her father, John Hull Morrison, III, at
Opening Hunt, Blue Ridge Hunt, 1990

Untitled

The greyhound
had a hangnail
and lost his race
because chasing
the rabbit
split him
into the quick

Part Five

Requiem

On Approaching the Shenandoah Valley

Paris mist
and foggy treeline
assault thine weary eyes.
A steeper hill
'til exhilaration
and RPMs swell.
Deer, cattle, sheep,
fuzzy mammalian dots
loom life over the quaint Paris Parish.
And we grow to bursting,
crest the brink
and slide from beauty
to glorious Shenandoah.

Tootie

I rode Tootie today
Slick coat
Dark liquid eyes
petite feet
Brush of mane and tail
Snappy movements
Rolicky rhythm
Soft loving lips
Nurturing nuzzles.

August 1993

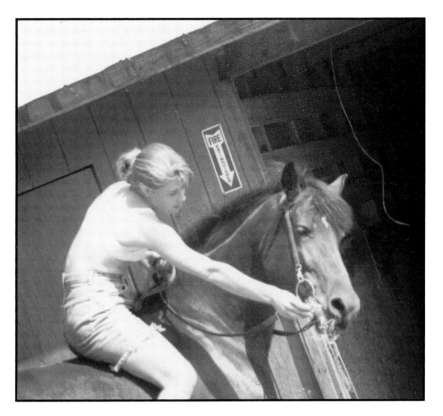

Kelly and Tootie

The Saga of Tootie (continues)

I went north to ride my horse
In a very uppity hunt meet

All they did was watch and stare
At Tootie's exquisite round hard feet

Her strong back, sloping shoulder
Honey eyes, fine coat, hot blooded heat

Rising through delicate rays
Rendering the dry air like Scotch, neat

Burning and refreshing like
Brazen envy from those of great feats.

Like mine, buying my young steed
For less than the knacker gives for meat.

October 1993

My Pony

My pony my love
Thou art as a dove
Flying wings above the night
Where the proud clouds
and June moon fight.
First the moon takes light
on the pillar of shrouds
Themselves the proud.
Then they cheat him
with a sleight of hand
and steal his precious
bright o'er the land
They push and shove.

September 1993

Spices

My grandmother
used to make these pickles
sweet pickles
thick, crunchy pieces
of clove
mixed in but then picked out.
At every family dinner
her pickles shone
And disappeared before the meal.

Now Thanksgiving
and the nursing home
doesn't allow canning
or making pickles.
And Grandma's illness
hangs like sticky
pickle juice over
our dinner
on the pretty lace tablecloth.

Kelly and her maternal grandmother, Mrs. Hazel Ryan.

For Brian Hill

He'd never been North.
North of Charlottesville
at least
not in a plane, or a train
or even a car.
We flew north – his neck
craned to see
the mountain range
of the Blue Ridge
We drove east – his eyes searching to find
the pointy tip
of the Capitol Building.
We drove West – over the Paris mountain, and
my eyes filled and
heart beat with pride
when he saw the
Valley, and I told
him it was my home.

Winter 1992

Kelly with Brian Hill of Ridgeville, South Carolina.

Roommate Arguments

Roommate arguments suck.
About baggies
books on the table
overfluxed ashtrays
incense ashes all over
screen door open
flies coming in
cat litter unchanged
rug burned and stained
(my mother's rug)
Bottles of booze
lying vacant
table overrun by stems
dried flowers shedding
petals and clumps
of dog hair, bird seed
moisture condensed
in rings under glasses
staining the coffee table
from her dead neighbor's
immaculate apartment.

September 1993

The Intellectual

Infinitesimal clouds drift through
between dust cover and book.
Lemonade rings saturate the
tabletops and stain.
Belt loop missed opens to an
endless field of possibilities.
The map of China looms over the austere room
White hands, not working man's hands,
flutter over the shelves of
priceless volumes.
It seems a crime for time to go so slowly here,
a dreadful injustice to the intellectuality professed.

Big Sky Farm

I've ridden a few German horses before.
You really have to push them together.
Lots of leg, firm demanding hands.

They don't like to carry themselves;
Rather they lean on the inside rein
Bowing out to the outside bend.

Takes a fit rider to get impulsion
or lightness. That internal rhythm
Maintained parallel to suppleness.

But this one, this "fancy" horse,
of German blood and bone, seems
to just know what those others did not.

Riders

The mournful wind
dove curiously over the
grassy apex of the hill.
Our buoyant steps
lose their individuality
become a single
universal train through the meadow.

We light upon a small mound,
Pause to gaze at the surrounding rocks
Then warily turn toward the last meniscus of sun
about to betray the casual onlookers.

It disappears gradually, leaving us unfulfilled
desiring to feel again
the splendor's glow
of true natural genius.

Untitled

What am I doing walking alone
in the park at night?
I never should have gotten off the bus.
The guides said
there were cats out here,
big ones. Cougars, yep
and, God – we saw a herd of warthog boars
turning their waterhole into a pigsty.

But the night was worse.
Only the smell and the splashing
Interrupt the stealthy paws,
Nails ticking on concrete.

County Fair

The tickets for
the rides and
the confectionary sugar
piled on the craggy dough
of the funnel cake
stuck to the
printers' ink
and tractor grease
on my father's
lined hands
like the Mexican
carny's flitting
grey eyes, scalding through
the scant bluejeans covering
my still hairy young legs
that carry me
toward the midway.

Untitled

Last night in the moments my thoughts were adrift
in coasting a terrace approaching a rift
through which I could spy several glimpses beneath
of the darkness, the light from above could not reach
I spied wings of reason herself taking flight
and upon yonder crescent he saw her alight
and glare back at me one look of dismay
She was the last one she thought I'd betray.

Someone the better, I said to myself
and jumped quite close to the top of the shelf.
I struggled with destiny upon the ledge
and gasped when defeated he slipped off the edge
And silence contagious in moments like these
consumed me and strengthened my will to appease
the passion that sparked me one terrible night
and shocked and persuaded my soul to ignite.

Kelly with the Clemson University tiger mascot

Requiem

Clemson Squirrels

The bristly tail
and swooping neckline
dip and dive into coarse
clipped grass
like a stray grey
goose on wobbly
wings, pecking
for food
fallen, forgotten
by the blue sign from the class of '44.

April 1994

Mr. Squirrel

Mr. Squirrel
Washing your nose
Outside the window
Tearing me
From memorable discussion
on Melville, Hawthorne.
Please stay,
Let me into your idyllic life
Jump down the tree
Scoop me up and make me your wife.
Take me out of here,
Fourth floor maze of senior haze.

Andy

That poundy feeling
when the phone rings…
you pick it up
and hear the voice
of a trillion flowers blooming.
Peace comes to you.
Your aura sits to rest your heart's hungry grumbling.
Pulls you back to the tenderness of the moments past.

Bed

First my lover took off his clothes
Then ruined the mood
and blew his nose.

Sick because it's cold outside,
Now under the covers –
I've a place to hide.

Midnight Daydream

To fall asleep on his chest
Entwine my body around his muscled one
Him hold me, and caress me, and
arouse me; sending waves of need
all through me, entering me
and making me need him.

Him to lick and tease and fulfill
To leave me shivering and lonely
Then return hot, and warm me again.
Warm me to kisses, tendernesses
Sweet nothingnesses
arrived at my door
Bursting in, shouting, cursing, frenzied
and calming, senses heightened
Crying for an end to torture.

Chains released, we escape
Together murmuring our love to the sheets.

1992

The Changing Face of Love

I'd always had that love for him.
Now it was pitted against him.
Would he survive? Is
that passion he has sturdy enough, daring enough,
southern rebel enough
to take me on
to take himself on
let mutual things take over –
dependence
friends
money
emotions
language
feelings?

Love is Not Always Enough

"Love is not enough sometimes. You need friend-
ship, caring, respect, compassion, and independence
when trying to love someone else and be apart of
their life. Just because you love someone doesn't
mean that everything will necessarily work out."

Journey Entry
November 19, 1993

Me As Hostess

Standing before the bay window
peeling paternal potatoes
Granny feeling the fruit
for the ambrosia
and all the women clucking
the men hollering at linemen
cousins galavanting on the lawn.

Wiping hands on cow apron
I return to splendor
as hostess.

November 1993

Paces of Living

Lights of cars in small towns
move slower
than those of cars in the big metropoli.

They trudge dutifully to their
destinations
While the rats in the city race
scurry to their caves.

A slow methodical routine
will always overrule
a frantic one.

Love Like An Arbor Grows

Love like an arbor grows
Around the wooden slats it goes
Tendrils winding in and through
Back and down, I love you.

Ever so slowly the thickness forms
More and more the desire warms
Desire to join, desire to mesh
spirit, mind, heart and flesh.

Branches close in, binding tight
Shutting out the harshest light.
Only small shafts shining in
Enough to keep the warmth in.

The warmth of two loves
Never to be scorned
Symbols of doves
with love they're adorned.

Nesting together atop the trellis
no need their love to embellish
Joined at last and forever
Hearts not parted, not ever.

November 1993
For the wedding of Christine and Mark

Kelly and her cousin, Christine Fuller Norin.

My Talent

"Up all night working on papers – the last thing I want to do now is dedicate any more time to this talent I have. If I'm so talented, why doesn't God zap me a printed, hard-bound copy of my next book complete with an order form for printing?"

Except from Journey Entry
November 1993

(Excerpt from a letter to the editor of *The Chronicle,* Clemson University's literary magazine)

..."The other problem that I have with *The Chronicle* is the lack of information relayed to the Clemson University public about submissions and deadlines. As an English/Sociology double major, it would seem that I might hear something on the winds of departmental gossip about where to send my poems or drawings. As a struggling young poet, I would die to be published, even in Clemson's small-time magazine. In my three years at Clemson, however, I have had two poems in one issue of *The Chronicle* two years ago."

..."As a poet and a student who pays partially for *The Chronicle's* circulation, I would appreciate the opportunity to submit works without relying on my random selection of classes whose attendance sheets include your name."

April 27, 1994

Fragments of Time

Filtered fragments of time
make their way down,
down through the ink
of my smiling pen
that then frowned
to see squiggles
from long ago
appear and build,
replicating the
chaotic microcosm
of twenty-year
grey-green mush.

No Time

People in every direction
No words exchanged,
No time to exchange them.

April 1994

My Maker

I glide
on the fibres
of light
from the peak
of the sky.
It's a small
stretch
to see my maker dethroned, perched
in a communications dish.
They said his beard would be flowing
white. But who
could know of
the Black Raiders cap
pulled low over
his eyes, keeping
out believers
defiled by time and twisted
versions of Genesis.

Elastic or Plastic

That slightly residual feeling
When you tear a band aid from
your scaly wound.
The still adhesive
hairless sensation as you
run your fingers over it,
a sting that subsides
then aches and returns to
a vague place on your leg.

Career Opportunities

It's easy to be a poet,
Sometimes you don't even know it.
A twist of the wrist, and you could be a great novelist,
Or write children's books with pretty cover looks.

Create a steamy romance, or teach readers to dance.
Think up jingles for singles, or do ads for modern fads.

Compose cereal box backs, don't get lax!
Keep on writing, come out of the dark,
You could always think up cards for Hallmark.

Write words to a song, or a play that's too long.
Form a plot for a movie; it could be groovy,
Or write for *People*, "Madonna at the Steeple."
People is creative, and journalism too,
But don't plan to make money, you genius you.

You could write for *The Sun, The Star* or *The Times*.
The Inquirer, Hard Copy and cover the grime.

Write articles freelance on ways to line dance,
Enter Hell infernal, join a literacy journal.

Help a small-time paper report small-time capers.
Or apply at *U.S. News and World Report.*
Their articles are usually pretty short.

Explore your options, don't give in,
You too can find a job with a little sin.
Your brain is a device
so hold out for your price.

Enjoy your talent and take a hint,
Creativity grows like a big ball of lint.

Goats

"I saw a field full of goats today. Probably about sixty goats of all different colors and sizes were in a beautiful green field that spaciously runs down a sloping hill to a semi-dried up spring that still feeds a trickle of algae-laden water. The goats were black and white and brown and white with floppy ears and shaggy bottoms.

"Goats are so free. Some people would love to have a dog's life – or perhaps a bird's flight, but I'd much rather be a goat in that meadow with my clan from generations back."

Journal Entry
September 1993

Dreams

"When I can't sleep at night I think of what will one day be. My pony – Tootie – with smiling kids – Hull and McRae – on her back trotting around placidly and tolerantly, bits of carrot falling out of her mouth from the instant in the field when the kids yelled for me to bring a carrot. They can't catch the pony. Jumping – flying – to my own memories of childhood, and Silver – my own pony – running from me in the field – me yelling for a carrot so I could catch him to trot placidly along with orange slobber on his lips."

Journal Entry
September 1993

I Shall Not Live in Vain

If I can stop one heart from breaking
I shall not live in vain.
If I can ease one life the aching,
or cool one pain,

Or help one fainting robin
onto his nest again,
I shall not live in vain.

November 1993

Kelly with Jay Darnell of Madison, Georgia, July 1994